THE ROASTING AND GRILLING COOKBOOK

100 PORK, BEEF, CHICKEN & SEAFOOD RECIPES

JACK HILL

All rights reserved.

Disclaimer

The information contained i is meant to serve as a comprehensive collection of strategies that the author of this eBook has done research about. Summaries, strategies, tips and tricks are only recommendation by the author, and reading this eBook will not guarantee that one's results will exactly mirror the author's results. The author of the eBook has made all reasonable effort to provide current and accurate information for the readers of the eBook. The author and it's associates will not be held liable for any unintentional error or omissions that may be found. The material in the eBook may include information by third parties. Third party materials comprise of opinions expressed by their owners. As such, the author of the eBook does not assume responsibility or liability for any third party material or opinions. Whether because of the progression of the internet, or the unforeseen changes in company policy and editorial submission guidelines, what is stated as fact at the time of this writing may become outdated or inapplicable later.

The eBook is copyright © 2022 with all rights reserved. It is illegal to redistribute, copy, or create derivative work from this eBook whole or in part. No parts of this report may be reproduced or retransmitted in any reproduced or retransmitted in any forms whatsoever without the writing expressed and signed permission from the author.

INTRODUCTION..8
PORK..10

1. Pork Collar and Rosemary Marinade 10
2. Roasted Ham 12
3. Smoked Pork Loin 14
4. Strawberry and Jalapeno Smoked Ribs 16
5. Easy Pork Chuck Roast 18
6. Jalapeno-Bacon Pork Tenderloin 20
7. Smoked Brats 22
8. Country Pork Roast 24
9. Pickled-Pepper Pork Chops 26
10. Southern-Sugar Glazed Ham 28
11. Bacon and Sausage Bites 30
12. Grilled Pork Chops 32
13. Pigs in a Blanket 34
14. Smoked Bacon 36
15. Smoked, Candied, and Spicy Bacon 37
16. St. Louis BBQ Ribs 39
17. Stuffed Pork Crown Roast 41
18. BBQ Baby Back Ribs 43
19. Pork Tenderloin 45
20. Apple Orange Pork Loin Roast 47
21. Pork Bone-In Chops with Rosemary and Thyme 49
22. Pork Ribs Smoked with Pomegranate Sauce 51
23. Hot and Tender Pork Sausage Balls 53
24. Pepper Jelly Pork Ribs 55
25. Pork Neck and Northwest Bean Soup 57
26. Smoked Pork Tenderloins 59
27. Pulled Hickory-Smoked Pork Butts 61
28. Pork Sirloin Tip Roast Three Ways 63
29. Smoked Pork Sausage 65
30. BBQ Pulled Pork 67
31. Smoked Bologna 69
32. Smoked Pork Shoulder 71
33. Spiced Pork Loin 73
34. Stuffed Porchetta 75
BEEF 77

35. Texas Smoked Brisket (Unwrapped) 77
36. Mesquite-Smoked Brisket (Wrapped) 79
37. Sweet Heat Burnt Ends 81
38. Reverse-Seared Tri-Tip 83
39. George's Smoked Tri-Tip 85
40. Beefy Bolognese 87
41. Brunch Burger 89
42. Classic Pastrami 91
43. Fully Loaded Beef Nachos 93
44. Whole Smoked Bologna Roll 95
45. Honey-Apple BBQ Ribs 97
46. Smoked Rib-Eye Steaks 99
47. Texan-Style Smoke Beef Brisket 101
48. Blackened Saskatchewan Tomahawk 103
49. BBQ Brisket 105
50. Beef Fajitas 107

POULTRY 109
51. Cajun Patch Cock Chicken 109
52. Yan's Grilled Quarters 111
53. Roasted Tuscan Thighs 113
54. Teriyaki Smoked Drumstick 115
55. Smoked Bone In-Turkey Breast 117
56. Smoked Whole Duck 119
57. Chicken Tenders 121
58. Thanksgiving Turkey 123
59. Spatchcock Smoked Turkey 125
60. Smoked Chicken Leg Quarters 127
61. Lemon Garlic Smoked Chicken 129
62. Sweet Honey Smoked Brown Turkey 131
63. Spicy Smoked Chicken Garlic 133
64. Hot Smoked Shredded Chicken 135
65. White Smoked Chicken Breast 137
66. Barbecue Chicken 139
67. Whole Turkey 141
68. Barbecue Chicken Breasts 143

69. Cilantro-Lime Chicken 145
70. Lemon Honey Chicken 147
71. Herbed Coffee Chicken... 149
72. Red Pepper Chicken Thighs 151

FISH AND SEAFOOD.. 153
73. Candied Smoked Salmon with Orange Ginger Rub153
74. Juicy Lime Smoked Tuna Belly................................. 155
75. Lemon Butter Smoked Mackerel with Juniper Berries Brine 157
76. Smoked Crab 159
77. Cayenne Garlic Smoked Shrimp 161
78. Cinnamon Ginger Smoked Crab 163
79. Simple Grilled Oysters... 165
80. Garlic Asiago Oysters... 167
81. Wasabi Oysters 169
82. Fish Camp Trout 171
83. Southern-Grilled Bass 173
84. Pacific Northwest Salmon with Lemon Dill Sauce175
85. Seared Wasabi Tuna 177
86. Bacon Grilled Crappie.. 179
87. Mojo Shrimp Skewer Appetizers 181
88. Sweet Grilled Lobster Tails 183
89. Seasoned Smoked Oysters...................................... 185
90. Sugar-Crusted Red Snapper.................................... 187
91. Peppercorn-Dill Mahi-Mahi 189
92. Fish Tacos with Fiery Peppers................................. 191
93. Honey-Cayenne Sea Scallops 193
94. Lemon Butter Lobster Tails 195
95. Smoked Fresh Salmon fillets 197
96. Caribbean Smoked Rockfish 199
97. Smoked Shrimp Tilapia.. 201
98. Smoked Brined Tuna 203
99. Smoked Sauced Tuna... 205
100. Smoked Brined Trout 207

CONCLUSION 209

INTRODUCTION

Welcome to the BBQ cookbook!

You're about to embark upon an adventure that is not only fun, but maybe even a little addicting. One thing's for sure, though: It's delicious!

You're new to grilling? You're afraid to light a barbecue? Well, have no fear. It's not as complicated as it looks. This book has got some recipes ready to go and some even call for indoor grilling!

What is BBQ?

Barbecue originated from the Caribbean word 'barbacoa', which is a native Indian structure used for smoking meats.

It's important to note that grilling and barbecuing are two different concepts. While grilling uses high and direct heat for quick cooks (think burgers, hot dogs, and steak), Barbecuing, on the other hand, requires indirect, consistent, low heat and longer cook times. Barbecuing also uses different types of smoke wood for an additional layer of flavour on top of the charcoal smoke. Meat used for BBQ is also tends to have a higher fat content, which provides tenderization and flavour over a long cooking time.

Tips to get you started:

- To avoid losing juices during turning, always flip your meat or vegetables using tongs or a spatula.

- Don't press down anything with a spatula while they're grilling! This squeezes out the juices.
- For great smoky flavour, soak some wood chips in water.
- To infuse grilled foods with herb essence, toss herbs directly onto the charcoal while you're grilling.

PORK

1. Pork Collar and Rosemary Marinade

Preparation Time: 15 minutes

Ingredients:
- 1 pork collar, 3-4 pounds
- 3 tablespoons rosemary, fresh
- 3 shallots, minced
- 2 tablespoons garlic, chopped
- ½ cup bourbon
- 2 teaspoons coriander, ground

- 1 bottle of apple ale
- 1 teaspoon ground black pepper
- 2 teaspoons salt
- 3 tablespoons oil

Directions:

Take a zip bag and add pepper, salt, canola oil, apple ale, bourbon, coriander, garlic, shallots, and rosemary and mix well

Cut meat into slabs and add them to the marinade, let it refrigerate overnight

Pre-heat your smoker to 450 degrees F

Transfer meat to smoker and smoke for 5 minutes, lower Smoke Temperature to 325 degrees F

Pour marinade all over and cook for 25 minutes more until the internal Smoke Temperature reaches 160 degrees F

2. Roasted Ham

Ingredients:

- 8-10 pounds ham, bone-in
- 2 tablespoons mustard, Dijon
- ¼ cup horseradish
- 1 bottle BBQ Apricot Sauce

Directions:

Pre-heat your smoker to 325 degrees F

Cover a roasting pan with foil and place the ham, transfer to smoker and smoke for 1 hour and 30 minutes

Take a small pan and add sauce, mustard, and horseradish, place it over medium heat and cook for a few minutes

Keep it on the side

After 1 hour 30 minutes of smoking, glaze ham and smoke for 30 minutes more until the internal Smoke Temperature reaches 135 degrees F

Let it rest for 20 minutes, slice and enjoy!

3. Smoked Pork Loin

Ingredients:
- ½ quart apple juice
- ½ quart apple cider vinegar
- ½ cup of sugar
- ¼ cup of salt
- 2 tablespoons fresh ground pepper
- 1 pork loin roast
- ½ cup Greek seasoning

Directions:
Take a large container and make the brine mix by adding apple juice, vinegar, salt, pepper, sugar, liquid smoke, and stir

Keep stirring until the sugar and salt have dissolved and added the loin

Add more water if needed to submerge the meat

Cover and chill overnight

Pre-heat your smoker to 250 degrees Fahrenheit with hickory Preferred Wood Pellet

Coat the meat with Greek seasoning and transfer to your smoker

Smoker for 3 hours until the internal Smoke Temperature of the thickest part registers 160 degrees Fahrenheit

4. Strawberry and Jalapeno Smoked Ribs

Ingredients:
- 3 tablespoons salt & Pepper
- 2 tablespoons ground cumin
- 1 tablespoon dried oregano
- 1 tablespoon garlic, minced
- 2 teaspoons chili powder
- 1 teaspoon celery seed
- 1 teaspoon dried thyme
- 1 rack spareribs
- 2 slabs baby back pork ribs
- 1 cup apple juice
- 2 jalapeno peppers
- ½ cup beer

- ½ cup onion, chopped
- ¼ cup sugar-free strawberry
- 3 tablespoons BBQ sauce
- 1 tablespoon olive oil
- 2 garlic cloves

Directions:

Place your baby back rib slabs and spare rib rack on sheets of aluminum foil and rub the spice mix all over their body

Divide and pour the apple juice amongst the foil packets and foil the edges together to seal them up

Cook on your smoker until the surface of your meat is finely dried up, it should take about 5-10 minutes.

5. Easy Pork Chuck Roast

Ingredients:

- 1 whole 4-5 pounds chuck roast
- ¼ cup olive oil
- ¼ cup firm packed brown sugar
- 2 tablespoons Cajun seasoning
- 2 tablespoons paprika
- 2 tablespoons cayenne pepper

Directions:

Pre-heat your smoker to 225 degrees Fahrenheit using oak Preferred Wood Pellet

Rub chuck roast all over with olive oil

Take a small bowl and add brown sugar, paprika, Cajun seasoning, cayenne

Coat the roast thoroughly with the spice mix

Transfer the chuck roast to smoker rack and smoke for 4-5 hours

6. Jalapeno-Bacon Pork Tenderloin

Ingredients:
- ¼ cup yellow mustard
- 2 (1-pound) pork tenderloins
- ¼ cup Our House Dry Rub
- 8 ounces cream cheese, softened
- 1 cup grated Cheddar cheese
- 1 tablespoon unsalted butter, melted
- 1 tablespoon minced garlic
- 2 jalapeño peppers, seeded and diced
- 1½ pounds bacon

Directions:

Slather the mustard all over the pork tenderloins, then sprinkle generously with the dry rub to coat the meat.

Place the tenderloins directly on the grill, close the lid, and smoke for 2 hours.

In a small bowl, combine the cream cheese, Cheddar cheese, melted butter, garlic, and jalapeños.

Spread half of the cream cheese mixture in the cavity of tenderloin.

Securely wrap tenderloin with half of the bacon. Repeat with the remaining bacon and the other piece of meat.

Transfer the bacon-wrapped tenderloins to the grill, close the lid, and smoke for about 30 minutes.

7. Smoked Brats

Ingredients:
- 4 (12-ounce) cans of beer
- 2 onions, sliced into rings
- 2 green bell peppers, sliced into rings
- 2 tablespoons unsalted butter, plus more for the rolls
- 2 tablespoons red pepper flakes
- 10 brats, uncooked
- 10 hoagie rolls, split
- Mustard, for serving

Directions:

Bring the beer, onions, peppers, butter, and red pepper flakes to a boil.

Place a disposable pan on one side of grill, and pour the warmed beer mixture into it, creating a "brat tub"

Place the brats on the other side of the grill, directly on the grate, and close the lid and smoke for 1 hour, turning 2 or 3 times.

Add the brats to the pan with the onions and peppers, cover tightly with aluminum foil, and continue smoking with the lid closed for 30 minutes to 1 hour.

Butter the cut sides of the hoagie rolls and toast cut side down on the grill.

Using a slotted spoon, remove the brats, onions, and peppers from the cooking liquid and discard the liquid.

8. Country Pork Roast

Ingredients:
- 1 (28-ounce) jar or 2 (14.5-ounce) cans sauerkraut
- 3 Granny Smith apples, cored and chopped
- ¾ cup packed light brown sugar
- 3 tablespoons Greek seasoning
- 2 teaspoons dried basil leaves
- Extra-virgin olive oil, for rubbing
- 1 (2- to 2½-pound) pork loin roast

Directions:

In a large bowl, stir together the sauerkraut, chopped apples, and brown sugar.

Spread the sauerkraut-apple mixture in the bottom of a 9-by-13-inch baking dish.

In a small bowl, mix the Greek seasoning and dried basil for the rub.

Oil the pork roast and apply the rub, then place it fat-side up in the baking dish, on top of the sauerkraut.

Transfer the baking dish to the grill, close the lid, and roast the pork for 3 hours.

9. Pickled-Pepper Pork Chops

Ingredients:
- 4 (1-inch-thick) pork chops
- ½ cup pickled jalapeño juice or pickle juice
- ¼ cup chopped pickled (jarred) jalapeño pepper slices
- ¼ cup chopped roasted red peppers
- ¼ cup canned diced tomatoes, well-drained
- ¼ cup chopped scallions
- 2 teaspoons poultry seasoning
- 2 teaspoons salt
- 2 teaspoons freshly ground black pepper

Directions:

Pour the jalapeño juice into a large container with a lid. Add the pork chops, cover, and marinate in the refrigerator for at least 4 hours or overnight, supplementing with or substituting pickle juice as desired.

In a small bowl, combine the chopped pickled jalapeños, roasted red peppers, tomatoes, scallions, and poultry seasoning to make a relish. Set aside.

Remove the pork chops from the marinade and shake off any excess. Discard the marinade. Season both sides of the chops with the salt and pepper.

Arrange the pork chops directly on the grill, close the lid, and smoke for 45 to 50 minutes.

10. Southern-Sugar Glazed Ham

Ingredients:
- 1 (12- to 15-pound) whole bone-in ham, fully cooked
- ¼ cup yellow mustard
- 1 cup pineapple juice
- ½ cup packed light brown sugar
- 1 teaspoon ground cinnamon
- ½ teaspoon ground cloves

Directions:

Preheat, with the lid closed, to 275°F.

Trim off the excess fat and skin from the ham, leaving a ¼-inch layer of fat. Put the ham in an aluminum foil-lined roasting pan.

On your kitchen stove top, in a medium saucepan over low heat, combine the mustard, pineapple juice, brown sugar, cinnamon, and cloves and simmer for 15 minutes, or until thick and reduced by about half.

Baste the ham with half of the pineapple-brown sugar syrup, reserving the rest for basting later in the cook.

Place the roasting pan on the grill, close the lid, and smoke for 4 hours.

Baste the ham with the remaining pineapple-brown sugar syrup and continue smoking with the lid closed for another hour. Serve

11. Bacon and Sausage Bites

Ingredients:

- Smoked sausages - 1 pack
- Thick-cut bacon - 1 lb.
- Brown sugar - 2 cups

Directions:

Slice ⅓ of the sausages and wrap them around small pieces of sausage. Use a toothpick to secure them.

Line a baking tray with baking paper and place the small pieces of wrapped sausage on it.

Sprinkle brown sugar on top.

Preheat the pellet to 300 degrees.

Keep the baking tray with the wrapped sausages inside for 30 minutes.

Remove and let it stay outside for 15 minutes.

Serve warm with a dip of your choice.

12. Grilled Pork Chops

Ingredients:

- Pork chops - 6, thickly cut
- Barbeque mix

Directions:

Preheat your pellet grill to 450 degrees.

Place the seasoned chops on the grill. Close the lid.

Cook for 6 minutes. The Smoke Temperature should be around 145 degrees when you remove the lid.

Remove the pork chops.

Let it remain open for 5-10 minutes.

Serve with your choice of side dish.

13. Pigs in a Blanket

Ingredients:

- Pork sausages - 1 pack
- Biscuit dough - 1 pack

Directions:

Preheat your pellet grill to 350 degrees.

Cut the sausages and the dough into thirds.

Wrap the dough around the sausages. Place them on a baking sheet.

Grill with a closed lid for 20-25 minutes or until they look cooked.

Take them out when they are golden brown.

Serve with a dip of your choice.

14. Smoked Bacon

Ingredients:

- Thick cut bacon - 1 lb.

Directions:

Preheat your pellet grill to 375 degrees.

Line a considerable baking sheet. Place a single layer of thick-cut bacon on it.

Bake for 20 minutes and then flip it to the other side.

Cook for another 10 minutes or until the bacon is crispy.

Take it out and enjoy your tasty grilled bacon.

15. Smoked, Candied, and Spicy Bacon

Ingredients:

- Center-cut bacon - 1 lb.
- Brown sugar - ½ cup
- Maple syrup - ½ cup
- Hot sauce - 1 tbsp
- Pepper - ½ tbsp

Directions:

Mix the maple syrup, brown sugar, hot sauce, and pepper in a bowl.

Preheat your pellet grill to 300 degrees.

Line a baking sheet and place the bacon slices on it.

Generously spread the brown sugar mix on both sides of the bacon slices.

Place the pan on the Pellet grill for 20 minutes. Flip the bacon pieces.

Leave them for another 15 minutes until the bacon looks cooked and the sugar is melted.

Remove from the grill and let it stay for 10-15 minutes.

16. St. Louis BBQ Ribs

Ingredients:

- pork as well as a poultry rubs - 6 oz
- St. Louis bone in the form of pork ribs - 2 racks
- Heat and Sweet BBQ sauce - 1 bottle
- Apple juice - 8 oz

Directions:

Apply an even coat of the poultry rub on the front and back of the ribs.

Preheat the pellet grill for around 15 minutes. Place the ribs on the grill grate, bone side down. Put the apple juice in an easy spray bottle and then spray it evenly on the ribs. Smoke the meat for 1 hour.

Remove the ribs from the pellet grill and wrap them securely in aluminum foil. Pour the remaining 6 oz of apple juice into the foil. Wrap it tightly.

Place the ribs on the grill again, meat side down. Smoke the meat for another 3 hours.

Once the ribs are done and cooked evenly, get rid of the foil. Gently brush a layer of the sauce on both sides of the ribs. Put them back on the grill to cook for another 10 minutes to ensure that the sauce is set correctly.

17. Stuffed Pork Crown Roast

Ingredients:
- 12-14 ribs
- Apple cider vinegar - 2 tbsp
- Apple juice - 1 cup
- Dijon mustard - 2 tbsp
- Salt - 1 tsp
- Brown sugar - 1 tbsp
- Freshly chopped thyme - 2 tbsp
- Cloves of minced garlic - 2
- Olive oil - ½ cup
- Coarsely ground pepper - 1 tsp

- Your favorite stuffing - 8 cups

Directions:

Use a pastry brush to apply the marinade to the roast.

Roast the meat for 30 minutes, and then reduce the Smoke Temperature of the grill. Fill the crown loosely with the stuffing and mound it at the top.

Roast the pork thoroughly for 90 more minutes.

Remove the roast from the grill. Allow it to rest for around 15 minutes so that the meat soaks in all the juices. Remove the foil covering the bones. Leave the butcher's string on until you are ready to carve it.

18. BBQ Baby Back Ribs

Ingredients:
- Baby back pork ribs - 2 racks
- Divided apple juice - ½ cup
- Yellow mustard - ⅓ cup
- BBQ sauce - 1 cup
- Worcestershire sauce - 1 tbsp
- Warmed honey - ⅓ cup
- Dark brown sugar - ½ cup
- Pork and poultry rub

Directions:

In a small bowl, combine ¼ cup of apple juice, the mustard, and the Worcestershire sauce. Spread the mixture on both sides of the pork ribs and season them with the pork and poultry rub.

Smoke the ribs for about 3 hours, meat-side up. Return all the foiled ribs back to the grill. Cook them for another 2 hours.

Remove the foil from the ribs and brush both sides with the BBQ sauce.

Continue grilling them for anywhere between 30-60 minutes until the sauce solidifies.

19. Pork Tenderloin

Ingredients:

- 1 Pork tenderloin GMG Pork Rub
- 1 Cup of Teriyaki Sauce

Directions:

You can use 1 to two pork tenderloins. Generously rub the pork tenderloins with the Green Mountain Pork Rub and let it stand aside for about 4 to 24 hours.

Set your Smoker grill at 320°F (160°C) and when the grill reaches the Smoke Temperature you are looking for, place in the tenderloin and baste both the sides with a sweet marinade like the Teriyaki sauce

Cook for about 1 and $\frac{1}{4}$ hours while turning frequently or just until the internal Smoke Temperature displays at least 165° F.

20. Apple Orange Pork Loin Roast

Ingredients:
- Peppercorns—6
- Pork loin—1 5lb.
- roast Orange juice—½ cup
- Lemon—1, halved
- Kosher salt—½ cup
- Fennel seeds—½ tsp.
- Brown sugar—¼ cup
- Olive oil—2 tbsps.
- Pepper flakes—½ tsp.
- Garlic—3 cloves
- Pepper and salt—as required

- Apple juice—½ cup
- Bay leaves 2
- Sauce

Directions:

In a large enough pot, prepare a mixture of brown sugar, salt, bay leaves, garlic, lemon, peppercorns, pepper flakes, fennel seeds, orange juice, and apple. Heat and simmer to dissolve sugar and salt.

In the cooled brine, add pork roast and submerge. Refrigerate for 8-12 hours.

Use olive oil to coat the roast and season with pepper and salt.

Roast the meat on the grilling grate for about 23-26 minutes. Serve with sauce.

21. Pork Bone-In Chops with Rosemary and Thyme

Ingredients:

- Butter—2 tbsps.
- Pork—4 chops, bone-in
- Rosemary—1 sprig
- Thyme—2 sprigs
- Pork rubs—according to taste

Directions:

Prepare your Smoker-Grill by preheating it to a Smoke Temperature of about 180°F. Close the top lid and leave for 12-18 minutes.

Use pork rub to coat the chops properly.

Transfer to the grilling grate and let the chops smoke for about 35-40 minutes. This should bring the internal Smoke Temperature to 130°F.

Remove and set aside the chops so they can cool down.

In a cast iron pan, combine the herbs, butter, and pork chops.

Sear the chops, 3-5 minutes on each side.

22. Pork Ribs Smoked with Pomegranate Sauce

Ingredients:
- Bay leaves 2
- Pork ribs—2 racks of baby back
- Cinnamon sticks 2
- Allspice berries—2 tbsps.
- Onion—1
- Salt—½ cup
- Whole peppercorns—2 tbsps.
- Garlic—1 head, halved
- Sauce

Directions:

Prepare the brine by combining water with bay leaves, garlic, allspice berries, onion, cinnamon sticks, peppercorn, and salt. Boil and then let the mixture cool.

Submerge the pork rib racks in the brine mixture. Cover and leave for 12-24 hours.

Put the bone section of the rib on the grilling grate. Smoke for about 2-3 hours coating regularly with the pomegranate sauce.

23. Hot and Tender Pork Sausage Balls

Ingredients:

For the meatballs:
- Whole milk—½ cup
- Pork sausage—½ lb., mild, ground
- Ground beef—2 ¼ lbs.
- Egg—1
- Chili powder—2 tsps.
- Breadcrumbs—1 cup
- Hot sauce—1 tsp.

Directions:

In a large enough mixing bowl, mix the ground sausage, beef, and breadcrumbs

In a different bowl, prepare a mixture of milk, hot sauce, and egg. Combine with the sausage mixture and add pepper, salt, and chili powder.

Prepare meatballs and place them on aluminum foil.

Put the meatballs in a cast iron pan and transfer to the grilling grate meatballs to smoke for about 48-60 minutes.

Remove the pan of smoked meatballs and pour the prepared sauce over them.

Cook the meatballs for about 35-45 minutes. Remove and serve with more sauce.

24. Pepper Jelly Pork Ribs

Ingredients:

- Sake—½ cup
- Pork ribs—2 racks of baby back, remove the membrane
- Garlic—4 cloves, crushed
- Orange juice—½ cup
- BBQ rub—4 tbsps.
- Fresh ginger—1 thumb, sliced
- Brown sugar—½ cup
- Hoisin sauce—1 cup
- Scallions—6, sliced
- Cayenne pepper—½ tsp.

- Soy sauce—$\frac{1}{2}$ cup
- Glaze

Directions:

Use the BBQ rub to coat the pork ribs and smoke on a pan on the grilling grate for about 60 minutes.

Prepare a mixture of soy sauce, hoisin sauce, orange juice, sake, cayenne, and brown sugar. Dissolve the sugar and add ginger and garlic.

Pour the prepared mixture over the pork ribs. Cover and seal the pan with aluminum foil.

Cook for around 3-4 hours. Remove and let the ribs rest.

25. Pork Neck and Northwest Bean Soup

Ingredients:

- Minced garlic—1 tbsp.
- Pork neck—1 1/2 lbs.
- Salt—1 tsp.
- Chicken stock—1 quart
- Bacon—3 slices, chopped
- Hot sauce—2 tsps.
- Northwest beans—2 cans
- Fresh parsley—1 tbsp., diced
- Yellow onion—1 large, diced

Directions:

Use salt and pepper to season the pork neck and transfer it to the grilling grate. Smoke for about 2 hours. Set aside the meat to let it cool.

Use a large enough pot to heat onions in oil and season with salt and pepper.

Add pork neck, hot sauce, and more salt to the cooked onions. Add water and bring to a boil in the smoker-grill, then simmer.

Cook on simmer for about 3-4 hours without covering the lid. Once cooled, pull the meat and shred.

Add the shredded meat and beans back into the soup mixture and heat thoroughly.

Serve with parsley and chopped bacon toppings.

26. Smoked Pork Tenderloins

Ingredients:

- 2 (1½ to 2-pound) pork tenderloins
- Cup roasted garlic-seasoned extra-virgin olive oil
- Dry Rub or Pork Dry Rub

Directions:

Rub sides of the tenderloins with the olive oil and residue with the rub.

Wrap the seasoned tenderloins in plastic coating and refrigerate for 2 to 4 hours.

Remove the plastic coating from the meat. Place the tenderloins on the grill and smoke them for 45 minutes at 230°F.

Increase the pit Smoke Temperature to 360°F and wrap up the tenderloins for around 45 other zone reaches 145°F.

Rest the pork tenderloins under a free foil tent for 10 minutes before serving.

27. Pulled Hickory-Smoked Pork Butts

Ingredients:

- 2 (10-pound) boneless pork butts, vacuum-stuffed or fresh
- 1 cup roasted garlic-seasoned extra-virgin olive oil
- ¾ cup Pork Dry Rub, Jan's Original Dry Rub, or your preferred pork rub

Directions:

Rub every one of the sides of every pork butt with the oil. Sprinkle every pork butt with a liberal measure of the rub and pat it in with your hand.

Smoke the pork butts for 3 hours.

Remove the pork butts and FTC them for 3 to 4 hours before pulling and serving.

Force the smoked pork butts into minimal succulent shreds utilizing your preferred pulling technique. I prefer utilizing my hands while wearing heat-safe gloves.

Serve the pulled pork with grill sauce on a fresh-prepared move topped with coleslaw.

28. Pork Sirloin Tip Roast Three Ways

Ingredients:

- ¾ cup 100% apple juice
- 2 tablespoons roasted garlic-seasoned extra-virgin olive oil
- 5 tablespoons Pork Dry Rub or a business rubs, for example, Plowboys BBQ Bovine Bold

Directions:

Utilize a flavor/marinade injector to infuse all zones of tip roast with the apple juice.

Rub the whole roast with the olive oil and afterward cover generously with the rub.

Roast the meat until the internal Smoke Temperature arrives at 145°F, about $1\frac{1}{2}$ hours.

Rest the roast under a free foil tent for 15 minutes.

29. Smoked Pork Sausage

Ingredients:
- 2 pounds pork butt, cubed
- 1/2-pound pork fat, cubed
- 1/2 teaspoon onion powder
- 1/2 teaspoon garlic powder
- 1 tablespoon sea salt
- 1 1/2 teaspoons ground black pepper
- 1 teaspoon brown sugar
- 1/4 teaspoon cayenne pepper
- 1 1/2 teaspoons dried oregano

- 1/4 cup water

Directions:

Take hog casings, place them in a large bowl, pour in water, and let soak for 1 hour.

Meanwhile, place pork butt and fat in a food processor, process until grind and place in a large bowl. Season with spices

Rinse hog casings, then working on one casing at a time, tie one end of the casing and another open end over the nozzle and slowly push meat mixture into the casing until filled.

Air dry the casing for 1 to 3 hours or rotate casing on paper towel often to dry its surfaces.

When ready to cook, place chilled sausage for 20 to 30 minutes

30. BBQ Pulled Pork

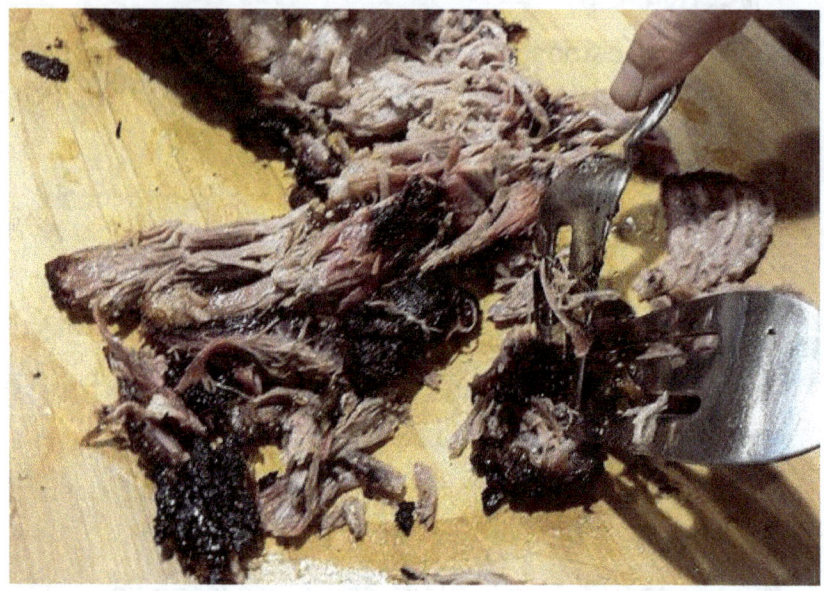

Ingredients:

- 8-pound pork butt roast, fat trimmed
- 2 tablespoons onion powder
- 2 tablespoons garlic powder
- 1/4 cup sea salt
- 1/2 cup brown sugar
- 1 tablespoon ground black pepper
- 1 tablespoon paprika
- 1 tablespoon dried thyme
- 1 tablespoon dried oregano
- 6 tablespoons yellow mustard BBQ sauce for serving

- Burger rolls for serving

Directions:

Rinse pork, pat dry and then rub with mustard.

Stir together remaining ingredients and sprinkle the spice mixture all over the pork until evenly coated.

Transfer pork roast into a foil pan, fat-side up, cover with plastic wrap and let marinate in the refrigerator for 8 to 12 hours.

Place pork on smoker rack, set the timer to smoke for 8 hours.

31. Smoked Bologna

Ingredients:

- 3 pounds bologna roll
- 2 tablespoons ground black pepper
- 3/4 cup brown sugar
- 1/4 cup yellow mustard

Directions:

Plug in the smoker, preheat smoker at 225 degrees F.

In the meantime, score bologna with $\frac{1}{4}$ inch deep diamond pattern, then coats with mustard and season with black pepper and sugar.

Place bologna on smoker rack, insert a meat thermometer, then shut with lid and set the timer to smoke for 3 to 4 hours.

32. Smoked Pork Shoulder

Ingredients:

- 8-pound pork shoulder roast, bone-in, and fat trimmed
- 2 teaspoons onion powder
- 2 teaspoons garlic powder
- 2 teaspoons celery salt
- 4 teaspoons salt
- 2 teaspoons ground black pepper
- 1/4 cup brown sugar
- 1/2 teaspoon cayenne pepper
- 1/2 cup paprika
- 2 teaspoons dry mustard

Directions:

Rinse pork shoulder, pat dry thoroughly with paper towels and place roast in a foil pan.

Stir together remaining ingredients until mixed and then season roast with the spice mixture until evenly coated.

Place pork on smoker rack to smoke for 8 hours.

When done, transfer pork to a cutting board, cover with aluminum foil and let rest for 30 minutes.

33. Spiced Pork Loin

Ingredients:

- 6-pound pork loin, boneless
- 1/2 teaspoon garlic powder
- 2 teaspoons sea salt
- 1 teaspoon ground black pepper
- 1 tablespoon Chinese five spice powder
- 2 tablespoons olive oil

Directions:

Rinse pork, pat dry with paper towels and place on a foil pan.

Stir together remaining ingredients until smooth paste form, then rub this paste on all sides of pork and let marinate for 60 minutes at room Smoke Temperature.

preheat smoker at 225 degrees F.

Place pork on smoker rack to smoke for 3 hours.

When done, transfer pork to a cutting board, cover with aluminum foil, and let rest for 30 minutes.

34. Stuffed Porchetta

Ingredients:

- 6 pounds pork belly, fat trimmed
- 12-ounce sundried tomato spread
- 2 cups giardiniera, Chicago styled
- 1 cup bacon jam
- ½ cup dry rub

Directions:

Preheat smoker at 275 degrees F.

In the meantime, rinse pork, pat dry and then season with dry rub on all sides until evenly coated.

Place seasoned pork on a cutting board or clean working space; spread tomato spread on top, layer with giardiniera and tomato spread, then roll pork and tie with kitchen twines.

Place stuffed pork on smoker rack, insert a meat thermometer, then shut with lid and set the timer to smoke for 2 to 3 hours or more until meat thermometer registers an internal Smoke Temperature of 195 degrees F.

When done, transfer porchetta to a cutting board, let rest for 15 minutes and then slice to serve.

BEEF

35. Texas Smoked Brisket (Unwrapped)

Ingredients:

- 1 (12-pound) full packer brisket
- 2 tablespoons yellow mustard
- 1 batch Espresso Brisket Rub
- Worcestershire Mop and Spritz, for spritzing

Directions:

Coat the brisket all over with mustard and season it with the rub. Using your hands, work the rub into the meat. Pour the mop into a spray bottle.

Place the brisket directly on the grill grate and smoke until its internal Smoke Temperature reaches 195°F, spritzing it every hour with the mop.

Pull the brisket from the grill and wrap it entirely in aluminum foil or butcher paper. Place the wrapped brisket in a more relaxed, cover the more relaxed, and let it rest for 1 or 2 hours.

Remove the brisket from the more relaxed and unwrap it.

36. Mesquite-Smoked Brisket (Wrapped)

Ingredients:

- 1 (12-pound) full packer brisket
- 2 tablespoons yellow mustard
- Salt
- Freshly ground black pepper

Directions:

Coat the brisket all over with mustard and season with salt and pepper.

Place the brisket directly on the grill grate and smoke until its internal Smoke Temperature reaches 160°F and the brisket has formed a dark bark.

Pull the brisket from the grill and wrap it entirely in aluminum foil or butcher paper.

Transfer the wrapped brisket to a calmer, cover the cooler, and let the brisket rest for 1 or 2 hours.

Remove the brisket from the more relaxed and unwrap it.

37. Sweet Heat Burnt Ends

Ingredients:

- 1 (6-pound) brisket point
- 2 tablespoons yellow mustard
- 1 batch Sweet Brown Sugar Rub
- 2 tablespoons honey
- 1 cup barbecue sauce
- 2 tablespoons light brown sugar

Directions:

Coat the point all over with mustard and season it with the rub. Using your hands, work the rub into the meat.

Place the point directly on the grill grate and smoke until its internal Smoke Temperature reaches 165°F.

Pull the brisket from the grill and wrap it entirely in aluminum foil or butcher paper.

Remove the point from the grill, unwrap it, and cut the meat into 1-inch cubes. Place the cubes in an aluminum pan and stir in the honey, barbecue sauce, and brown sugar.

Place the pan in the grill and smoke the beef cubes for 1 hour more, uncovered. Remove the burnt ends from the grill and serve immediately.

38. Reverse-Seared Tri-Tip

Ingredients:

- 1½ pounds tri-tip roast
- 1 batch Espresso Brisket Rub

Directions:

Season the tri-tip roast with the rub. Using your hands, work the rub into the meat.

Place the roast directly on the grill grate and smoke until its internal Smoke Temperature reaches 140°F.

Increase the grill's Smoke Temperature to 450°F and continues to cook until the roast's internal Smoke Temperature reaches 145°F. This same technique can be done over an open flame or in a cast-iron skillet with some butter.

Remove the tri-tip roast from the grill and let it rest 10 to 15 minutes, before slicing and serving.

39. George's Smoked Tri-Tip

Ingredients:

- 1½ pounds tri-tip roast
- Salt
- Freshly ground black pepper
- 2 teaspoons garlic powder
- 2 teaspoons lemon pepper
- ½ cup apple juice

Directions:

Season the tri-tip roast with salt, pepper, garlic powder, and lemon pepper. Using your hands, work the seasoning into the meat.

Place the roast directly on the grill grate and smoke for 4 hours.

Pull the tri-tip from the grill and place it on enough aluminum foil to wrap it completely.

Fold in three sides of the foil around the roast and add the apple juice. Fold in the far side, completely enclosing the tri-tip and liquid. Return the wrapped tri-tip to the grill and cook for 45 minutes more.

Remove the tri-tip roast from the grill and let it rest for 10 to 15 minutes, before unwrapping, slicing, and serving.

40. Beefy Bolognese

Ingredients:

- Ground beef (2-lbs, 0.9-kgs)
- Olive oil – 1 tablespoon
- 3 garlic cloves, minced
- 1 yellow onion, peeled and diced
- 3 large tomatoes, chopped
- Tomato sauce – 2 cups
- Dried oregano – 2 teaspoons
- Dried basil – 1 teaspoon
- Salt and black pepper
- Spaghetti (8-ozs, 227-gms)

- Salted butter – 1 tablespoon
- Parmesan cheese, grated

Directions:

First, heat the oil in a deep pan. Add the beef, garlic, and onion to the pan. Sauté until the beef browns, and the onion softens.

Add the tomatoes followed by the tomato sauce, oregano, basil, paprika, salt, and black pepper. Stir to combine. Bring to a simmer for 5 minutes and stir occasionally.

Take the pan off the stove and transfer it to the smoker. Smoke for 1-1½ hours stir occasionally.

In the meantime, cook the spaghetti using packet Directions: then drain.

41. Brunch Burger

Ingredients:
- Lean ground chuck beef (6-ozs, 170-gms)
- 4 rashers bacon, cooked until crispy
- Salt and black pepper
- Olive oil
- 2 burger buns
- 2 slices American cheese
- 2 medium eggs, fried
- 2 hash browns, cooked and kept warm

Directions:

Divide the beef into two portions and form into thin, even patties. Season with salt and black pepper.

Brush the grate with oil before placing the patties on top. Grill for 3-4 minutes each side until cooked to your preference.

Take the burgers off the grill and place each in a bun. Top each patty with a slice of cheese, bacon, followed by a fried egg and hash brown.

Serve straight away.

42. Classic Pastrami

Ingredients:

- Beef brisket, cut from the point
- Kosher salt – 6½ tablespoons
- Brown sugar – 6 tablespoons
- Coriander seeds – ¼ teaspoon
- Honey – 1 tablespoon
- 3 bay leaves, chopped
- Garlic, peeled and chopped – 1 teaspoon
- Cayenne pepper – ¼ teaspoon
- Whole black peppercorns – ¼ cup

- Brown sugar – 1 tablespoon
- Coriander seeds – ¼ cup
- Garlic powder – 2 teaspoons
- Paprika – 1 tablespoon
- Onion powder – 2 teaspoons

Directions:

Combine the kosher salt, brown sugar, coriander seeds, curing salt, honey, bay leaves, garlic, and cayenne pepper and transfer to a large container.

Add the meat to the cooled brine and weigh down with a plate. Set the meat aside for one week to brine.

In a bowl, combine the black peppercorns, brown sugar, coriander seeds, garlic powder, paprika, and onion powder. Rub the mixture evenly over the outside of the meat. Place the meat on the grill grate and cook for 4 hours.

43. Fully Loaded Beef Nachos

Ingredients:

- Ground beef (1-lbs, 0.45-kgs)
- 1 large bag tortilla chips
- 1 green bell pepper, seeded and diced
- Scallions, sliced – ½ cup
- Red onion, peeled and diced – ½ cup
- Cheddar cheese, shredded – 3 cups
- Sour cream, guacamole, salsa – to serve

Directions:

In a cast-iron pan, arrange a double layer of tortilla chips.

Scatter over the ground beef, bell pepper, scallions, red onion, and finally the cheddar cheese.

Place the cast-iron pan on the grill and cook for approximately 10 minutes until the cheese has melted completely.

Take off the grill and serve with sour cream, guacamole, and salsa on the side.

44. Whole Smoked Bologna Roll

Ingredients:

- Whole beef bologna roll (3-lbs, 1.4-kgs)
- Black pepper, freshly cracked – 2 tablespoons
- Brown sugar – ¾ cup
- Yellow mustard – ¼ cup

Directions:

Combine the black pepper and brown sugar.

Score the outside of the bologna with a diamond pattern.

Spread mustard over the outside of the bologna and then rub in the black pepper/sugar until thoroughly and evenly coated.

Arrange the bologna on the smoker's upper rack and cook for 3-4 hours until the outside caramelizes.

Slice the bologna into medium-thick slices and serve.

45. Honey-Apple BBQ Ribs

Ingredients:

- 4 slabs baby back ribs
- Paprika – ½ cup
- Brown sugar - ⅔ cup
- Onion powder – 2 tablespoons
- Garlic powder - ⅓ cup
- Cayenne pepper – 1 tablespoon
- Chili powder – 2 tablespoons
- White pepper – 1 tablespoon
- Black pepper – 1 tablespoon
- Ground cumin – 1½ teaspoons

- Dried oregano – 1½ teaspoons
- White grape juice – ½ cup
- Apple juice – ½ cup
- Honey
- BBQ sauce

Directions:

First, prepare the rub and Sprinkle the rub mixture evenly over the ribs on both sides.

Place the ribs on the hot grill, close the lid and cook for 45 minutes.

In the meantime, stir together the grape and apple juice and set to one side.

Pour the grape-apple juice over the ribs. Drizzle a generous amount of honey over the rubs. Wrap the ribs with the foil, sealing the edges tightly.

Return the ribs to the grill and cook for another hour.

46. Smoked Rib-Eye Steaks

Ingredients:

- 2 thick rib-eye steaks (1.5-lbs, 0.68-kgs)
- Salt and black pepper
- Steak rubs, of choice

Directions:

Allow the steaks to sit out at room Smoke Temperature for half an hour.

Season the steaks with salt, black pepper, and your choice of rub. Arrange the steaks directly on the grill and cook for just over 20 minutes.

Take the streaks off the grill and set the Smoke Temperature to 400°F (205°C).

Sear the cooked steaks on the hotter grill for 5 minutes on each side.

Wrap the steaks in kitchen foil and set aside for 10 minutes to rest.

Slice and serve with your choice of sides.

47. Texan-Style Smoke Beef Brisket

Ingredients:

- 1 whole packet brisket
- Sea salt – 2 tablespoons
- Garlic powder – 2 tablespoons
- Bblack pepper – 2 tablespoons

Directions:

In a bowl, combine the rub ingredients, sea salt, garlic powder and black pepper. Rub the seasoning all over the brisket.

Arrange the meat on the smoker with the pointed end facing towards the primary heat source. Close the smoker lid and smoke for approximately 8 hours.

Wrap the meat, by folding the foil edge over edge to create a leaf-proof seal all the way around. Return the foil-wrapped brisket to the smoker, seam side facing downwards.

Close the smoker's lid and continue to cook at 225°F (110°C). This will take between 5-8 hours.

48. Blackened Saskatchewan Tomahawk

Ingredients:
- 2 (40 Oz) Tomahawk Steaks
- 4 Tbsp Butter
- 4 Tbsp Blackened Saskatchewan Rub

Directions:

When ready to cook, set Smoke Temperature to 225°F and preheat, lid closed for 15 minutes. For optimal flavor, use Super Smoke if available.

Cover cold steaks in the Blackened Saskatchewan Rub. Let rest 10 minutes for the seasoning to adhere.

Place steaks directly on grill grates and smoke for about 40 minutes, or until an internal temp reaches 119°F. Remove from grill and wrap tightly in foil to rest. Turn up Smoke Temperature on the grill to 400°F - with a cast iron pan or griddle inside. When the pan is hot, add 2 Tbsp of butter and sear the first steak, about 2-4 minutes per side, or until the internal Smoke Temperature reads 125°F - 130°F

49. BBQ Brisket

Ingredients:

- 1 (12-14 Lb.) Whole Packer Brisket
- Beef Rub, As Needed

Directions:

Coat meat liberally with Beef Rub

When seasoned, wrap brisket in plastic wrap. Let the wrapped meat sit 12 to 24 hours in the refrigerator.

Place meat fat side down on the grill grate and cook for 6 hours

Place foiled brisket back on grill and cook until it reaches a finished internal Smoke Temperature of 204 this should take an additional 3-4 hours.

Remove from grill and allow to rest in the foil for at least 30 minutes. Slice. Enjoy!

50. Beef Fajitas

Ingredients:

- 2 pounds beef strips
- 1 large onion (sliced)
- 2 celery stalks (diced)
- 1 large red bell pepper (sliced)
- 1 large orange bell pepper (sliced)
- 1 green bell pepper (sliced)
- 2 tbsp lime juice
- 2 tsp cumin
- 2 tsp chili powder
- 1 tsp brown sugar

- ½ tsp paprika
- 1 tbsp olive oil
- 1 tsp salt
- ½ tsp ground black pepper

Directions:

In a large mixing bowl, combine the cumin, lime juice, salt, black pepper, paprika and sugar. Add the beef and toss to combine. Cover the bowl tightly with aluminum foil and refrigerate for 1 hour.

Place a skillet on the grill grate and add the oil. Add the onion, celery, red bell pepper, orange pepper and green bell pepper. Sauté until veggies are tender.

Arrange the beef strips onto the grill grate. Cook for about 12 minutes.

POULTRY

51. Cajun Patch Cock Chicken

Ingredients:

- 4-5 pounds of fresh or thawed frozen chicken
- 4-6 glasses of extra virgin olive oil
- Cajun Spice Lab 4 tablespoons or Lucile Bloody Mary Mix Cajun Hot Dry Herb Mix Seasoning

Directions:

Rub olive oil freely under and on the skin. Season chicken in all Directions: and apply directly to the meat under the skin.

Wrap the chicken in plastic wrap and place in the refrigerator for 3 hours to absorb the flavor.

Make chicken for 1.5 hours.

Place the chicken under a loose foil tent for 15 minutes before carving.

52. Yan's Grilled Quarters

Ingredients:

- 4 fresh or thawed frozen chicken quarters
- 4-6 glasses of extra virgin olive oil
- 4 tablespoons of Yang's original dry lab

Directions:

Cut off excess skin and fat chicken. Carefully peel the chicken skin and rub olive oil above and below each chicken skin.

In Jean's original dry lab, apply seasonings to the top and bottom of the skin and the back of the chicken house.

Wrap the seasoned chicken in plastic wrap and store refrigerated for 2-4 hours to absorb flavor.

Place chicken on grill and cook at 325 °F for 1 hour.

53. Roasted Tuscan Thighs

Ingredients:

- 8 chicken thighs, with bone, with skin
- 3 extra virgin olive oils with roasted garlic flavor
- 3 cups of Tuscan or Tuscan seasoning per thigh

Directions:

Lightly rub olive oil behind and below the skin and thighs. A seasoning from Tuscan, seasoned on the skin of the thigh and the top and bottom of the back.

Wrap chicken thighs in plastic wrap, refrigerate for 1-2 hours, and allow time for flavor to be absorbed before roasting.

Depending on the grill of the Smoker, roast for 40-60 minutes until the internal Smoke Temperature of the thick part of the chicken thigh reaches 180 ° F. Place the roasted Tuscan thighs under a loose foil tent for 15 minutes before serving.

54. Teriyaki Smoked Drumstick

Ingredients:

- 3 cup teriyaki marinade and cooking sauce like Yoshida's original gourmet
- Poultry seasoning 3 tsp
- 1 tsp garlic powder
- 10 chicken drumsticks

Directions:

In a medium bowl, mix the marinade and cooking sauce with the chicken seasoning and garlic powder.

Put the drumstick in a marinade pan or 1-gallon plastic sealable bag and pour the marinade mixture into the drumstick. Refrigerate overnight.

Place the skin on the drumstick and, while the grill is preheating, hang the drumstick on a poultry leg and wing rack to drain the cooking sheet on the counter. If you do not have a poultry leg and feather rack, you can dry the drumstick by tapping it with a paper towel.

After 1 hour, raise the hole Smoke Temperature to 350 ° F and cook the drumstick for another 30-45 minutes until the thickest part of the stick reaches an internal Smoke Temperature of 180 ° F.

55. Smoked Bone In-Turkey Breast

Ingredients:

- 1 (8-10 pounds) boned turkey breast
- 6 tablespoons extra virgin olive oil
- 5 Yang original dry lab or poultry seasonings

Directions:

Rub or season carefully under the chest cavity, under the skin and on the skin.

Place the turkey breast in a V-rack for secure handling or place it directly on a grill grate with the breast up.

Rest the turkey breasts on the kitchen counter at room Smoke Temperature and preheat the Smoker grill.

Smoke the boned turkey breast directly in a V rack or grill at 225 ° F for 2 hours.

After 2 hours of hickory smoke, raise the pit Smoke Temperature to 325 ° F. Roast until the thickest part of the turkey breast reaches an internal Smoke Temperature of 170 ° F and the juice is clear.

Place the hickory smoked turkey breast under a loose foil tent for 20 minutes, then scrape the grain.

56. Smoked Whole Duck

Ingredients:

- 5 pounds whole duck (trimmed of any excess fat)
- 1 small onion (quartered)
- 1 apple (wedged)
- 1 orange (quartered)
- 1 tbsp freshy chopped parsley
- 1 tbsp freshly chopped sage
- ½ tsp onion powder
- 2 tsp smoked paprika
- 1 tsp dried Italian seasoning

- 1 tbsp dried Greek seasoning
- 1 tsp pepper or to taste
- 1 tsp sea salt or to taste

Directions:

To make rub, combine the onion powder, pepper, salt, Italian seasoning, Greek seasoning and paprika in a mixing bowl.

Insert the orange, onion, and apple to the duck cavity. Stuff the duck with freshly chopped parsley and sage.

Season all sides of the duck generously with rub mixture.

Place the duck on the grill grate.

Roast for 2 to 21/2 hours, or until the duck skin is brown and the internal Smoke Temperature of the thigh reaches 160°F.

57. Chicken Tenders

Ingredients:

- 6 chicken tenders
- ¼ tsp granulated garlic (not garlic powder)
- ¼ tsp pepper
- 1 tsp paprika
- ½ tsp kosher salt
- 1 tbsp olive oil
- 1 tbsp lemon juice
- 1 tsp Italian seasoning
- 1 tbsp chopped parsley

Directions:

In a large mixing bowl, combine the garlic, pepper, salt, lemon, Italian seasoning and paprika. Add the chicken tenders and toss to combine. Cover the bowl and refrigerate for 1 hour.

Remove the chicken tenders from the marinade and let them rest for 1 hour, until the tenders are at room temperature. Pat dry with paper towels

Arrange the chicken tenders onto the grill and grill 8 minutes, 4 minutes per side.

58. Thanksgiving Turkey

Ingredients:

- 2 cups butter (softened)
- 1 tbsp cracked black pepper
- 2 tsp kosher salt
- 2 tbsp freshly chopped rosemary
- 2 tbsp freshly chopped parsley
- 2 tbsp freshly chopped sage
- 2 tsp dried thyme
- 6 garlic cloves (minced)
- 1 (18 pound) turkey

Directions:

In a mixing bowl, combine the butter, sage, rosemary, 1 tsp black pepper, 1 tsp salt, thyme, parsley, and garlic.

Use your fingers to loosen the skin from the turkey.

Generously, Rub butter mixture under the turkey skin and all over the turkey as well. 4. Season turkey generously with herb mix. 5. Preheat the grill to 300°F with lid closed for 15 minutes.

Place the turkey on the grill and roast for about 4 hours, or until the turkey thigh Smoke Temperature reaches 160°F.

Remove the turkey from the grill and let it rest for a few minutes.

Cut into sizes and serve.

59. Spatchcock Smoked Turkey

Ingredients:

- 1 (18 pounds) turkey
- 2 tbsp finely chopped fresh parsley
- 1 tbsp finely chopped fresh rosemary
- 2 tbsp finely chopped fresh thyme
- ½ cup melted butter
- 1 tsp garlic powder
- 1 tsp onion powder
- 1 tsp ground black pepper
- 2 tsp salt or to taste
- 2 tbsp finely chopped scallions

Directions:

In a mixing bowl, combine the parsley, rosemary, scallions, thyme, butter, pepper, salt, garlic, and onion powder.

Rub butter mixture over all sides of the turkey.

Preheat your grill to HIGH (450°F) with lid closed for 15 minutes.

Place the turkey directly on the grill grate and cook for 30 minutes. Reduce Preferred Wood Pellet to 300°F and cook for an additional 4 hours.

Remove the turkey from the grill and let it rest for a few minutes.

Cut into sizes and serve.

60. Smoked Chicken Leg Quarters

Ingredients:

- 8 chicken leg quarters
- 2 tbsp olive oil
- 1 tsp salt or to taste
- ½ tsp chili powder
- ½ tsp paprika
- ½ tsp ground thyme
- 1 tsp dried rosemary
- ½ tsp cayenne pepper
- 1 tsp garlic powder
- 1 tsp onion powder

Directions:

To make rub, combine cayenne, rosemary, garlic, onion powder, chili, paprika, salt and thyme.

Drizzle oil over the chicken leg quarters and season the quarters generously with rub mix.

Arrange the chicken onto the grill grate. Smoke for 1 hour, flipping halfway through.

Cook for an additional 1 hour.

Remove chicken from grill and let it rest for about 15 minutes.

Serve and enjoy.

61. Lemon Garlic Smoked Chicken

Ingredients:

- Whole Chicken (3-lbs., 1.4-kg.)
- The Brine
- Salt – ½ cup
- Brown sugar – 1 cup
- Water – 3 ½ liters

The Rub

- Minced garlic – ¼ cup
- Garlic powder – 2 tablespoons
- Lemon juice – 3 tablespoons
- Paprika – 2 ½ tablespoons

- Chili powder – 2 tablespoons
- Thyme – ¾ tablespoon
- Cayenne – 2 tablespoons
- Salt – 1 tablespoon
- Black pepper – 2 tablespoons

The Filling

- Chopped onion – 1 cup
- Garlic – 5 cloves
- Thyme – 5 sprigs

Directions:

Place chicken in brine overnight.

Combine the rub ingredients & Rub the chicken with the spice mixture then fill the cavity with chopped onion, garlic, and thyme.

Smoke the chicken for approximately 3 hours.

62. Sweet Honey Smoked Brown Turkey

Ingredients:

- Whole Turkey (6-lbs., 2.7-kg.)
- Salt – 5 tablespoons
- Brown sugar – 5 tablespoons
- Thyme – 1 tablespoon
- Chopped rosemary – 1 tablespoon
- Sage – 1 tablespoon
- Black pepper – 2 ½ teaspoons
- Garlic powder – 2 teaspoons
- Raw honey – 1 cup
- Brown sugar – 3 tablespoons
- Apple Cider Vinegar – 2 tablespoons

- Mustard – ¾ tablespoon
- Salt – 1 teaspoon
- Pepper – 2 teaspoons

Directions:

Combine the rub ingredients & Rub the turkey with the spice mixture then let it rest for a few minutes.

Smoke the turkey for approximately 4 hours.

Quickly place brown sugar, apple cider vinegar, mustard, salt, and pepper in a bowl then pour raw honey over the mixture. Stir until combined.

Baste the smoked turkey with the honey mixture then return it to the Smoker.

63. Spicy Smoked Chicken Garlic

Ingredients:

- Whole Chicken (3-lbs., 1.4-kg.)
- Salt – 1 teaspoon
- Paprika – 1 teaspoon
- Garlic powder – 1 ½ teaspoons
- Black pepper – 1 ½ teaspoons
- Red chili flakes – 2 teaspoons
- Cayenne pepper – ½ teaspoon
- Thyme – ¾ teaspoon
- Oregano – ½ teaspoon
- Brown sugar – 3 tablespoons

Directions:

Rub the chicken with salt, paprika, garlic powder, black pepper, red chili flakes, cayenne pepper, thyme, oregano, and brown sugar.

Wrap the seasoned chicken with plastic wrap then let it rest for approximately an hour. Store in the fridge to keep it fresh

Smoke the chicken for approximately 3 hours.

Cut the smoked chicken into pieces then serve.

64. Hot Smoked Shredded Chicken

Ingredients:

- Boneless Chicken breast (3-lbs., 1.4-kg.)
- Paprika – 3 tablespoons
- Chili powder – 3 tablespoons
- Thyme – 1 ½ tablespoons
- Garlic powder – 1 ½ tablespoons
- Onion powder – 1 ½ tablespoons
- Cayenne – 3 tablespoons
- Salt – 1 ½ tablespoons
- Black pepper – 1 ½ tablespoons

- Honey - ½ cup
- Maple syrup - ¼ cup
- Brown sugar - 2 tablespoons

Directions:

Combine the rub ingredients and rub with the spice mixture. Let it rest for a few minutes.

Smoke the chicken for an hour then transfer to a disposable aluminum pan.

Quickly combine honey with maple syrup then stir until incorporated.

Drizzle half of the honey mixture over the chicken breast then sprinkle brown sugar on top.

Place the disposable aluminum pan with chicken inside in the Pellet smoker then smoke for about 2 hours.

65. White Smoked Chicken Breast

Ingredients:

- Boneless Chicken breast (4.5-lbs., 2 -kg.)
- Vegetable oil – 3 tablespoons
- Chicken broth – ¼ cup
- Worcestershire sauce – 2 tablespoons
- Salt – ¾ tablespoon
- Garlic powder – 1 ½ teaspoons
- Onion powder – 1 ½ teaspoons
- Bay leaf – ¾ teaspoon
- Thyme – ¾ teaspoon
- Sage – ¾ teaspoon

- Black pepper – ¾ teaspoon
- Salt – 2 tablespoons
- Minced garlic – 3 tablespoons
- Minced ginger – 1 tablespoon
- Lemon juice – 3 tablespoons

Directions:

Pour vegetable oil and chicken broth into a bowl then season with Worcestershire sauce, salt, garlic powder, onion powder, bay leaf, thyme, sage, and black pepper. Stir the liquid until incorporated.

Fill an injector with the liquid mixture then inject the chicken breast at several places.

After that, combine the rub ingredients & Rub the chicken breast with the spice mixture then let it rest for an hour.

Smoke the chicken for 2 hours.

66. Barbecue Chicken

Ingredients:

- 8 Chicken breasts
- Two t. salt
- Two c. barbecue sauce, divided
- Two t. garlic powder
- Two t. pepper

Directions:

Add Preferred Wood Pellet pellets to your smoker and follow your cooker's startup procedure. Preheat your smoker, with your lid closed, until it reaches 250.

Rub the chicken with the spices and lay in a roasting pan. Cover the chicken before placing them on the grill. For about two hours, let them smoke. It should reach 165. During the last 15 minutes, baste with a c. of barbecue sauce.

Serve with the rest of the sauce.

67. Whole Turkey

Ingredients:
- Two t. thyme
- Two t. sage
- ½ c. apple juice
- One stick melted butter
- ¼ c. poultry seasoning
- 10-12-pound turkey

Directions:

Add Preferred Wood Pellet pellets to your smoker and follow your cooker's startup procedure. Preheat your smoker, with your lid closed, until it reaches 250.

Rub the oil and seasoning on the turkey. Get some in under the skin as well as inside.

Mix the thyme, sage, juice, and butter.

Place the turkey in a roasting pan, put it on the grill, cover, and cook 5-6 hours. Baste it every hour with the juice mixture. It should reach 165. Let it rest for 15-20 minutes before carving.

68. Barbecue Chicken Breasts

Ingredients:

- Two T. Worcestershire sauce
- ½ c. hot barbecue sauce
- One c. barbecue sauce
- Two cloves minced garlic
- ¼ c. olive oil
- 4 chicken breasts

Directions:

Put the chicken breasts into a deep container.

In another bowl, put the Worcestershire sauce, barbecue sauces, garlic, and olive oil. Stir well to combine.

Use half to marinate the chicken and reserve the rest for basting.

Add Preferred Wood Pellet pellets to your smoker and follow your cooker's startup procedure. Preheat your smoker, with your lid closed, until it reaches 350.

Take the chicken breasts out of the sauce. On the grill, place them before smoking them for approximately 20 minutes.

About ten minutes before the chicken is finished, baste with reserved barbecue sauce.

69. Cilantro-Lime Chicken

Ingredients:
- Pepper
- Salt
- 4 cloves minced garlic
- ½ c. lime juice
- One c. honey
- Two T. olive oil
- ½ c. chopped cilantro
- 4 chicken breasts

Directions:

Put the chicken breasts into a large zip-top bag.

In another bowl, put the pepper, salt, olive oil, garlic, honey, lime juice, and cilantro. Stir well to combine.

Use half as a marinade and reserve the rest for later.

Place into the refrigerator for four to five hours.

Remove the chicken breasts the bag. Use paper towels to pat them dry. Let them smoke up in the grill for about fifteen mins.

About five minutes before the chicken is finished, baste with reserved marinade.

70. Lemon Honey Chicken

Ingredients:
- Pepper
- Salt
- Chopped rosemary
- One clove crushed garlic
- One T. honey
- Juice of one lemon
- ½ c. chicken broth
- 3 T. butter
- 4 chicken breasts

Directions:

Place a pan on the stove and melt the butter. Place chicken breasts into hot butter and sear on each side until a nice color has formed.

Take out of the pan and allow resting for ten minutes.

In a small bowl, put the pepper, salt, rosemary, garlic, honey, lemon juice, and broth. Stir well to combine.

Rub each breast with the honey lemon mixture.

Put the chicken breasts onto the preheated grill and grill for 20 minutes.

71. Herbed Coffee Chicken

Ingredients:
- Salt
- ¾ c. strong brewed coffee
- One t. coriander seeds
- 4 lemon slices
- One t. peppercorns
- One t. mustard seeds
- ½ c. chicken broth
- ¼ c. dark brown sugar, packed
- Two T. melted butter

- 4 chicken breast halves

Directions:

Rub the butter on the chicken and rub in the salt.

In an enormous container, stir together the remaining ingredients. Cover the chicken with marinade.

Place into the refrigerator for two hours.

Add Preferred Wood Pellet pellets to your smoker and follow your cooker's startup procedure. Preheat your smoker, with your lid closed, until it reaches 350.

Smoke the chicken for ten minutes. There is no need to flip. Serve.

72. Red Pepper Chicken Thighs

Ingredients:

- One T. garlic powder
- One t. curry powder
- One t. red pepper flakes
- One t. black pepper
- Two T. olive oil
- ½ c. chicken broth
- One t. oregano
- One t. paprika
- Two pounds chicken thighs

Directions:

Put the chicken thighs into a large flat dish in a single layer.

In a bowl, put the olive oil, garlic powder, curry, oregano, pepper, paprika, red pepper flakes, and broth. Stir well to combine.

The mixture should be poured on top of the chicken.

Let the chicken marinate for four hours.

Add Preferred Wood Pellet pellets to your smoker and follow your cooker's startup procedure. Preheat your smoker, with your lid closed, until it reaches 450.

The chicken thighs should be removed from the bag. Use paper towels to pat them dry. Place them onto the preheated grill with the skin down and smoke for ten minutes. Turnover and cook for an additional ten minutes.

FISH AND SEAFOOD

73. Candied Smoked Salmon with Orange Ginger Rub

Ingredients:

- Salmon fillet (4-lbs., 1.8-kg.)

The Marinade

- Brown sugar – ¼ cup
- Salt – ½ teaspoon

The Rub

- Minced garlic – 2 tablespoons
- Grated fresh ginger – 1 teaspoon

- Grated orange zest – ½ teaspoon
- Cayenne pepper – ½ teaspoon

The Glaze
- Red wine – 2 tablespoons
- Dark rum – 2 tablespoons
- Brown sugar – 1 ½ cups
- Honey – 1 cup

Directions:

Mix salt with brown sugar then apply over the salmon fillet.

Rub the salmon fillet with the spice mixture then set aside.

Place the seasoned salmon in Pellet smoker and smoke for 2 hours.

Mix red wine with dark rum, brown sugar, and honey then stir until dissolved. Baste.

74. Juicy Lime Smoked Tuna Belly

Ingredients:

- Tuna belly (3-lb., 1.4-kg.)
- The Marinade
- Fresh limes – 2
- White sugar – 2 tablespoons
- Brown sugar – 3 tablespoons
- Pepper – ½ teaspoon
- Soy sauce – 1 tablespoon
- Sriracha sauce – 2 tablespoons

Directions:

Marinate the tuna belly with the juice for 10 minutes.

Meanwhile, combine white sugar with brown sugar, pepper, soy sauce, and Sriracha sauce then mix well.

Wash and rinse the tuna belly then pat it dry.

Wait until the Pellet smoker reaches the desired Smoke Temperature then place the seasoned tuna belly in it.

Smoke the tuna belly for 2 hours or until it flakes and once it is done, remove it from the Smoker.

75. Lemon Butter Smoked Mackerel with Juniper Berries Brine

Ingredients:

- Mackerel fillet (4-lbs., 1.8-kg.)

The Brine

- Cold water – 4 cups
- Mustard seeds – 1 tablespoon
- Dried juniper berries – 1 tablespoon
- Bay leaves – 3
- Salt – 1 tablespoon

The Glaze

- Butter – 2 tablespoons

- Lemon juice – 2 tablespoons

Directions:

Pour cold water into a container then season with salt, bay leaves, dried juniper berries, and mustard seeds then stir well.

Add the mackerel fillet to the brine mixture then soak. Place the salted mackerel on a sheet of aluminum foil then baste butter over it.

Drizzle lemon juice then wrap the mackerel fillet with the aluminum foil.

Smoke the wrapped mackerel for 2 hours or until it flakes and once it is done, remove from the Smoker.

76. Smoked Crab

Ingredients:

- Fresh Crabs (7-lb., 3.2-kg.)

The Sauce

- Salt – 1 tablespoon
- Cayenne pepper – 1 ½ teaspoons
- Salted butter – 2 cups
- Lemon juice – ½ cup
- Worcestershire sauce – 1 tablespoon
- Garlic powder – 2 teaspoons
- Smoked paprika – 2 teaspoons

Directions:

Preheat a saucepan over low heat then melt the butter. Let it cool.

Season the melted butter with salt, cayenne pepper, Worcestershire sauce, garlic powder, and smoked paprika then pour lemon juice into the melted butter. Stir until incorporated and set aside.

Arrange the crabs in a disposable aluminum pan then drizzle the sauce over the crabs.

Smoke the crabs for 30 minutes then remove from the Smoker.

77. Cayenne Garlic Smoked Shrimp

Ingredients:

- Fresh Shrimps (3-lb., 1.4-kg.)

The Spices

- Olive oil – 2 tablespoons
- Lemon juice – 2 tablespoons
- Salt – ¾ teaspoon
- Smoked paprika – 2 teaspoons
- Pepper – ½ teaspoon
- Garlic powder – 2 tablespoons
- Onion powder – 2 tablespoons
- Dried thyme – 1 teaspoon
- Cayenne pepper – 2 teaspoons

Directions:

Combine salt, smoked paprika, pepper, garlic powder, onion powder, dried thyme, and cayenne pepper then mix well. Set aside.

Drizzle olive oil and lemon juice over the shrimps and shake to coat. Let the shrimps rest for approximately 5 minutes.

Sprinkle the spice mixture over the shrimps then stir until the shrimps are entirely seasoned.

Place the disposable aluminum pan with shrimps in the Pellet smoker and smoke the shrimps for 15 minutes. The shrimps will be opaque and pink.

Remove the smoked shrimps from the Pellet smoker and transfer to a serving dish.

Serve and enjoy.

78. Cinnamon Ginger Smoked Crab

Ingredients:

- Fresh Crabs (7-lb., 3.2-kg.)

The Spices

- Salt – 1 tablespoon
- Ground celery seeds – 3 tablespoons
- Ground mustard – 2 teaspoons
- Cayenne pepper – ½ teaspoon
- Black pepper – ½ teaspoon
- Smoked paprika – 1 ½ teaspoons
- Ground clove – A pinch

- Ground allspice – ¾ teaspoon
- Ground ginger – 1 teaspoon
- Ground cardamom – ½ teaspoon
- Ground cinnamon – ½ teaspoon
- Bay leaves – 2

Directions:

Combine the whole spices & Sprinkle the spice mixture over the crabs then wrap the crabs with aluminum foil.

Place the wrapped crabs in the Pellet smoker and smoke for 30 minutes.

Once it is done, remove the wrapped smoked carbs from the Pellet smoker and let it rest for approximately 10 minutes.

Unwrap the smoked crabs and transfer it to a serving dish.

79. Simple Grilled Oysters

Ingredients:
- 4 dozen oysters, scrubbed
- Lemon wedges
- 1 C butter
- 1 Tsp seasoned salt
- 1 tsp lemon pepper

Directions:

Preheat pellet grill to 350F.

Melt butter with seasoned salt and lemon pepper, mixing well. Simmer 10 minutes.

Place oysters, unshelled, on pellet grill.

When shells pop open (3-5 minutes), use an oyster knife to detach oyster from top shell, and plop it back into the cup with the hot oyster liquor. Discard the lid.

Add a teaspoon of seasoned butter and serve.

80. Garlic Asiago Oysters

Ingredients:
- 1 lb. sweet cream butter
- 1 Tbsp. minced garlic
- 2 dozen fresh oysters
- ½ C. grated Asiago cheese
- French bread, warmed
- ¼ cup chives, diced

Directions:

Start pellet grill and heat to medium high.

Melt butter over medium-high heat. Reduce heat to low and stir in garlic.

Cook 1 minute and remove from heat.

Place oysters, cup down, on pellet grill. As soon as shells pop open, remove from grill.

Shuck oysters, keeping as much of the oyster liquor in place as possible.

Cut connective muscle and return each oyster to its shell.

Drizzle each oyster with 2 teaspoons butter mixture and sprinkle with 1 teaspoon cheese. Grill over high heat 3 minutes or until cheese browns. Sprinkle with chives.

Remove from pellet grill and serve immediately with bread and remaining butter on the side.

81. Wasabi Oysters

Ingredients:

- 12 small Pacific oysters, raw in shell 2 Tbsp. white wine vinegar
- 8 oz white wine 1/4 C shallots, minced
- 2 Tbsp. wasabi mustard 1 Tbsp. soy sauce
- 1 C unsalted butter, cubed 1 C chopped cilantro leaves
- Salt and black pepper to taste

Directions:

In a saucepan, over medium heat, combine the white wine vinegar, wine, and shallots. Simmer until the liquid is slightly reduced. Add wasabi mustard and soy sauce, stirring.

Over low heat gradually whisks in butter. Do not let the mixture boil. stir in cilantro, and remove from heat.

Cook oysters until shells just open. Remove oysters from the pellet grill and cut the connective muscle from the top shell,

Press each oyster (in shell) into the coarse salt to keep it upright, then spoon 1-2 teaspoons of wasabi-butter sauce over each and serve immediately.

82. Fish Camp Trout

Ingredients:

- 4 small whole trout, cleaned
- 4 strips of bacon
- 4 sprigs of fresh thyme
- 1 lemon
- salt and pepper to taste

Directions:

Oil grates and preheat pellet grill. Fry bacon, so that it is started to cook, but is still soft. Rinse out the trout and pat dry with a paper towel.

Place a sprig of thyme inside each fish. Wrap each trout with a strip of bacon and secure with a toothpick.

Place trout on pellet grill or in an oiled grill basket, and grill 5-7 minutes per side depending on the size of the trout. The trout is done when the meat turns opaque in the center and easily flakes.

Squeeze a little fresh lemon juice over each fish and serve.

83. Southern-Grilled Bass

Ingredients:
- 2 lbs. bass fillets or steaks
- 1 C. mayonnaise
- 4 oz. soy sauce

Directions:

Mix mayonnaise and soy sauce.

Cover entire surface (meat side) of each bass fillet with mixture.

Place on pellet grill, skin-side down. Do not turn.

When edges turn up and scales flake, remove and serve.

84. Pacific Northwest Salmon with Lemon Dill Sauce

Ingredients:
- 6lb Chinook salmon fillets
- Salt to taste
- 1 C butter, melted
- 1 C lemon juice
- 4 Tbsp. dried dill weed
- 1 Tbsp. garlic salt
- Black pepper to taste
- 4 C plain yogurt

Directions:

Place salmon fillets in a baking dish.

Mix the butter and 1/2 lemon juice in a small bowl, and drizzle over the salmon. Season with salt & pepper.

Combine yogurt, dill, garlic powder, sea salt, and pepper. Spread sauce evenly over salmon.

Quickly wipe hot pellet grill grate with a towel dipped in a little canola oil, place fillets on grill, tent with foil, and close lid.

Grill fish, skin down, to medium rare, about 6 minutes.

85. Seared Wasabi Tuna

Ingredients:

- 6-ounce tuna steaks
- 1 1/4 cup white wine
- 1 cup cilantro leaves
- 1 cup unsalted butter
- 1/4 cup shallots, minced
- 2 Tbsp. white wine vinegar
- 1 tablespoon wasabi paste
- 1 tablespoon soy sauce
- 1 tablespoon olive oil
- salt and pepper to taste

Directions:

Combine wine, wine vinegar and shallots in a saucepan over medium heat. Simmer to reduce to about 2 tablespoons. Strain out the shallots and discard.

Add wasabi and soy sauce to mixture and reduce Preferred Wood Pellet. Slowly add butter while stirring until thoroughly mixed. Stir in cilantro and remove from heat. Set aside.

Brush tuna steaks with olive oil. Season with salt and pepper and place on grill.

Grill for 90 seconds then turn and continue grilling for 90 seconds more.

86. Bacon Grilled Crappie

Ingredients:

- 20 Crappie Fillets
- 20 Bacon Slices
- ¼ teaspoon garlic powder
- ¼ teaspoon onion powder
- ¼ teaspoon pepper

Directions:

Sprinkle spices on fillets. Roll up fillets, wrap with bacon and peg with a toothpick.

Grill over meager heat, with apple Preferred Wood Pellet pellets, turning fillets several times.

Be sure to put out all flames caused by bacon grease with a water spray bottle.

Cook until bacon is brown and inside of fillet flakes.

87. Mojo Shrimp Skewer Appetizers

Ingredients:
- 2 lbs. sliced bacon
- 64 raw prawns, tail off
- 2 C Traditional Cuban Mojo
- ¼ C Adobo Criollo
- 32 Preferred Wood Pellet skewers, soaked

Directions:

Rinse raw prawns and drain. In a large bowl, toss prawns and Adobo Criollo spices.

Wrap each prawn in ½ slice of bacon, and thread two wraps onto each skewer, touching, and with skewer through both the bacon and the shrimp.

Bring pellet grill to medium heat, oil, and lay skewers in grill.

Grill 3-5 minutes, until bacon is cooked, flip, and cook 2-3 more minutes.

Remove from grill and let rest on a paper-towel covered platters 2-3 minutes before serving. for this type of grilling.

88. Sweet Grilled Lobster Tails

Ingredients:

- 12 lobster tails
- ½ C olive oil
- ¼ C fresh lemon juice
- ½ C butter
- 1 Tbsp. crushed garlic
- 1 tsp sugar
- 1/2 tsp salt
- ½ tsp black pepper

Directions:

Combine lemon juice, butter, garlic, salt, and pepper over med-low heat and mix until well blended, keep warm.

Create a "cool zone" at one end of the pellet grill. Brush the meat side of tails with olive oil, place onto grill and cook for 5-7 minutes, depending on the size of the lobster tail.

After turning, baste meat with garlic butter 2-3 times.

The shell should be bright red when they are finished. Remove the tails from the grill, and using large kitchen shears, cut the top part of the shell open.

Serve with warm garlic butter for dipping.

89. Seasoned Smoked Oysters

Ingredients:

- ½ cup soy sauce
- 2 tablespoons Worcestershire sauce
- 1 cup firmly packed brown sugar
- 2 dried bay leaves
- 2 garlic cloves, minced
- 2 teaspoons salt and black pepper
- 1 tablespoon hot sauce
- 1 tablespoon onion powder
- 2 dozen raw, shucked oysters
- ¼ cup olive oil

- ½ cup (1 stick) unsalted butter
- 1 teaspoon garlic powder

Directions:

In a large container, mix the water, soy sauce, Worcestershire, salt, sugar, bay leaves, garlic, pepper, hot sauce, and onion powder.

Submerge the raw oysters in the brine and refrigerate overnight.

Place the oysters on a non-stick grill mat, drizzle with the olive oil, and place the mat in the smoker.

Smoke the oysters for 1½ to 2 hours, until firm. Serve with the butter and garlic powder.

90. Sugar-Crusted Red Snapper

Ingredients:

- 1 tablespoon brown sugar
- 2 teaspoons minced garlic
- 2 teaspoons salt
- 2 teaspoons freshly ground black pepper
- ½ teaspoon crushed red pepper flakes
- 1 (1½- to 2-pound) red snapper fillet
- 2 tablespoons olive oil, plus more for oiling the grate
- 1 sliced lime, for garnish

Directions:

Following the manufacturer's specific start-up procedure, preheat the smoker to 225°F, and add alder Preferred Wood Pellet.

In a small bowl, mix the brown sugar, garlic, and salt, pepper, and red pepper flakes to make a spice blend.

Rub the olive oil all over the fish and apply the spice blend to coat.

Oil the grill grate or a nonstick grill mat or perforated pizza screen. Place the fillet on the smoker rack and smoke for 1 to 1½ hours, until the internal Smoke Temperature registers 145°F.

Remove the fish from Preferred Wood Pellet and serve hot with the lime slices.

91. Peppercorn-Dill Mahi-Mahi

Ingredients:

- 4 mahi-mahi fillets
- ¼ cup chopped fresh dill
- 2 tablespoons freshly squeezed lemon juice
- 1 tablespoon crushed black peppercorns
- 2 teaspoons minced garlic
- 1 teaspoon onion powder
- 1 teaspoon salt
- 2 tablespoons olive oil

Directions:

Trim the fillets as needed, cutting out any visible red bloodline. It will not hurt you, but its more robust flavor can quickly permeate the rest of the fillet.

In a small bowl, whisk together the dill, lemon juice, peppercorns, garlic, onion powder, and salt to make a seasoning.

Rub the fish with the olive oil and apply the seasoning all over. Oil the grill grate or a nonstick grill mat or perforated pizza screen.

Place the fillets on the smoker rack and smoke for 1 to $1\frac{1}{2}$ hours.

92. Fish Tacos with Fiery Peppers

Ingredients:

- 1 (16-ounce) carton prepared sweet coleslaw
- 1 small red onion, chopped
- 1 poblano pepper, chopped
- 1 jalapeño pepper, chopped
- 1 serrano pepper, chopped
- ¼ cup chopped fresh cilantro
- 1 tablespoon minced garlic
- 2 teaspoons salt, divided
- 2 teaspoons freshly ground black pepper, divided

- 1 lime, halved
- 1-pound skinless cod, halibut, or any white fish (see tip)
- 1 tablespoon olive oil, plus more for oiling the grate
- Flour or corn tortillas
- 1 avocado, sliced thin

Directions:

Make the slaw.

Juice one half of the lime and cut the other half into wedges. Rub the fish all over with the lime juice and olive oil.

Season the fish & Place the fish on the smoker rack and smoke for 1 to $1\frac{1}{2}$ hours

93. Honey-Cayenne Sea Scallops

Ingredients:

- ½ cup (1 stick) butter, melted
- ¼ cup honey
- 2 tablespoons ground cayenne pepper
- 1 tablespoon brown sugar
- 1 teaspoon garlic powder
- 1 teaspoon onion powder
- ½ teaspoon salt
- 20 sea scallops (about 2 pounds)

Directions:

In a small bowl, whisk together the butter, honey, cayenne, brown sugar, garlic powder, onion powder, and salt.

Place the scallops in a disposable aluminum foil roasting pan and pour the seasoned honey butter over them.

Set the pan on the smoker rack and smoke the scallops for about 25 minutes, until opaque and firm and the internal Smoke Temperature registers 130°F.

Remove the scallops from Preferred Wood Pellet and serve hot.

94. Lemon Butter Lobster Tails

Ingredients:

- 4 (8-ounce) lobster tails, fresh (not frozen)
- 1 cup (2 sticks) unsalted butter, melted, divided
- Juice of 2 lemons
- 1 teaspoon minced garlic
- 1 teaspoon dried thyme
- 1 teaspoon dried rosemary
- 1 teaspoon salt
- 1 teaspoon freshly ground black pepper
- Olive oil, for oiling the grate
- ¼ cup chopped fresh parsley

Directions:

In a small bowl, whisk together the butter, lemon juice, garlic, thyme, rosemary, salt, and pepper. Baste each lobster tail with 1 tablespoon of lemon butter.

Place the tails on the smoker rack split-side up.

Smoke the tails for 45 minutes to 1 hour, basting each with 1 tablespoon of lemon butter once during cooking.

Remove the lobster tails & sprinkle with the parsley and serve with the remaining lemon butter for dipping.

95. Smoked Fresh Salmon fillets

Ingredients:

- 1 Salmon fillets (fresh, wild, skin on)
- 1/3 Teaspoon of Old Bay Seasoning
- 1 Teaspoon of Basic Seafood Seasoning

Directions:

Pepping for the Grill

Wash salmon fillets fish with cold water and use a paper towel to pat dry

Rub the seasoning on the salmon fillets lightly

Pepping on the Preferred Wood Pellet smoker

Set the Preferred Wood Pellet smoker grill to indirect cooking and preheat to 400°F

Place the fillets skin down directly on the grill grates

Smoke the salmon fillets in the smoker until the internal Smoke Temperature rises to 140°F and fork can easily flake the flesh

Allow the salmon resting for 5 minutes

Serve and enjoy

96. Caribbean Smoked Rockfish

Ingredients:

- 4 Ounces of Pacific Rockfish fillets
- 1 Tablespoon of Caribbean seafood seasoning
- 2 Teaspoons of extra virgin olive oil

Directions:

Rub olive oil to all sides of the rockfish fillets

Rub the seasoning on the salmon fillets lightly

Place the fillets skin down directly on the grill grates

Smoke the salmon fillets in the smoker until the internal Smoke Temperature rises to 140°F and fork can easily flake the flesh

Allow the salmon resting for 5 minutes

Serve and enjoy

97. Smoked Shrimp Tilapia

Ingredients:
- 3 Ounces Tilapia fillets (fresh, farmed)
- 3/4 Teaspoon of Paprika (smoked)
- 1 Tablespoon of extra virgin olive
- 3/4 Teaspoon of Seafood Seasoning

Ingredients for Shrimp Stuffing:
- 1/2 Pound of Tail-off Shrimp
- 1/2 Cup of Breadcrumbs
- 1/2 Tablespoon of salted Butter
- 3/4 Teaspoon of pepper
- 1 Egg (small, beaten)

- 1/4 Cup of mayonnaise
- 3/4 Teaspoon of Parsley (dried)

Directions:

Pour shrimps into a food processor to chop it finely

Heat olive over medium-high heat in a large skillet, adds butter and melts it, and adds onion and sauté until soft

Combine sautéed mixture, shrimp and the remaining ingredients in a bowl that has cover

Rub olive oil on all sides of the fillets. Use a spoon to stuff some great stuffing on the back of each fillet.

Spread the stuffing on the back of the fillets

Fold the tilapia fillets into twos and use toothpicks to hold them tight.

Roast the fillets for 40 minutes

98. Smoked Brined Tuna

Ingredients:

- 3 Pounds of Salmon fillets (farmed)
- 2 Cups of Fresh fish Brine

Directions:

Cut the fillets into 4 inches sizes so to be able to cook at an equal rate

Put the pork chops into a sealable plastic container and pour into the container Fresh fish Brine

Cover it and place in the fridge overnight

After this duration remove the pork chops and pat dry with paper towels

Set the Smoker grill to indirect cooking

Transfer the salmon fillets into Teflon-coated fiberglass mat

Preheat the smoker to 180°F and cook until the internal Smoke Temperature of the salmon fillets rises to 145°F

99. Smoked Sauced Tuna

Ingredients:

- 10 Ounces Tuna Steaks (fresh)
- 1 Cup of Teriyaki sauce

Directions:

Cut the tuna into 4 inches sizes so to be able to cook at an equal rate

Put the tuna steaks into a sealable plastic container and pour into the container Teriyaki sauce

Cover it and place in the fridge for 3 hours

After this duration remove the tuna steaks and pat dry with paper towels

Transfer the fillet to nonstick grill tray and place in the smoker for 1 hour

After this time increase Preferred Wood Pellet to 250°F and cook until the internal Smoke Temperature of the tuna rises to 145°F

Remove them from the grill and allow resting for 10 minutes

Serve and enjoy

100. Smoked Brined Trout

Ingredients:

- 2 Whole Trout (fresh, skin on, pin bones removed)
- 3 Cups of Fresh fish Brine

Directions:

Put the trout into a sealable plastic container and pour into the container Fresh fish Brine

Transfer the fillet to nonstick grill tray and place in the smoker for 1 minute

Continue smoking until the internal he of the tuna rises to 145°F

Remove them from the smoker and allow resting for 5 minutes

Serve and enjoy

CONCLUSION

So now that we have reached the end of the book, I am very optimistic that you are well acquainted with some of the finest smoker grill recipes which will make you a pro at grilling, BBQ, and cooking in general.

Sometimes seeing so many recipes briefly can be very overwhelming. Therefore we had segmented this book into different sections each spanning recipes of a similar kind. So, go through the book as and when needed and make sure to follow the instructions in the recipe thoroughly.

www.ingramcontent.com/pod-product-compliance
Lightning Source LLC
Chambersburg PA
CBHW071825080526
44589CB00012B/918